Step This Way For Healing

by

Joseph Murphy

Step This Way For Healing
by Joseph Murphy

ISBN: 978-93-58592-64-1

Published by

DOUBLE 9 BOOKS

2/13-B, Ansari Road
Daryaganj, New Delhi – 110002
info@double9books.com
www.double9books.com
Tel. 011-40042856

ABOUT THE AUTHOR

Irish author and New Thought minister Joseph Denis Murphy (May 20, 1898 - December 16, 1981) was ordained in Divine Science and Religious Science. Irish author and New Thought minister Joseph Denis Murphy (May 20, 1898 - December 16, 1981) was ordained in Divine Science and Religious Science. Murphy was raised a Roman Catholic and was born in Ballydehob, County Cork, Ireland, the son of a private boys' school headmaster. He left his family behind to move to America in order to pursue his desire to learn new things and experience new things, which he was unable to accomplish in the Catholic-dominated Ireland. Murphy visited India and spent a lot of time studying Hinduism with Indian sages. Later, he established a new Hindu-inspired church in America. Over 30 books were authored by Murphy. The Power of Your Subconscious Mind, his most well-known book, was initially released in 1963. Millions of copies were sold globally when it quickly became a bestseller.

CONTENTS

Murphy on Quimby

Phineas Parkhurst Quimby once called on a woman who was aged, lame, bound down, and on crutches. He states that her ailment was due to the fact that she was imprisoned by a creed so small and contracted that she could not stand upright or move ahead. She was living in a tomb of fear and ignorance; furthermore, she was taking the Bible literally, and it frightened her. In this tomb, Quimby said, the presence of God was trying to burst the bars, break through the bands, and rise from the dead. When the woman would ask other people for an explanation of some passage of the Bible, the answer would be as a stone, and she would hunger for the bread of life. Dr. Quimby diagnosed her case as a mind cloudy and stagnated due to excitation and fear, caused by inability to see clearly the meaning of the scriptural passages she had been reading. This condition showed itself in her body by a heavy and sluggish feeling, which would terminate in paralysis.

Quimby asked the woman what was meant by, "Yet a little while I am with you, and then I go unto him that sent me." She replied that it meant that Jesus went to heaven. Quimby made plain what the passage really meant by interpreting that being with her "a little while" meant his explanation of her symptoms, feelings, and their cause - that is, he had compassion and sympathy for her momentarily, but he could not remain in that mental state; the next step was to go to "him that sent me," which is the presence of God in all men.

Quimby immediately traveled in his mind and contemplated perfect health, which is a part of God. He said to the woman, "Therefore, where I go, you cannot come, for you are in Calvin's belief, and I am in health." This explanation produced an instantaneous sensation in the woman, and a change came over her mind. She walked without her crutches. She had been, as it were, dead in error, and to bring her to life or truth was to raise her from the dead. "I quoted the resurrection of Christ and applied it to her own Christ or health; it produced a powerful effect on her" (The Quimby Manuscripts).

Apply this principle of healing in your own life. Suppose, for instance, that your son was sick. Go within to him who sent you. God, or Life, sent all of us into the world. God is all bliss, harmony, peace, beauty, wisdom, and perfection. Turn within in thought, and quietly realize that the wisdom and infinite intelligence of God are right within you. The living intelligence and power of God sent you into this world and fashioned all your organs from its own invisible pattern. You are now turning to the maker of your body. You are relaxed, at peace, poised and calm. You are full of confidence that the Creator of your body and mind can create and refashion your body according to his own divine pattern.

You have seen your son sick and in pain, but now in your meditation you are talking to the God-presence, calling forth the healing power. Think of your son, and immediately dwell on the peace, health, and harmony of God. You know that these qualities, potencies, and aspects of God are now being reflected in your boy. You are now getting into the mental atmosphere of health. As did Quimby, you are contemplating the Divine Ideal, which is perfection, wholeness, and harmony for your son. Do this frequently, three or four times daily, until you believe in the idea of perfect health. When you have mentally accepted the idea that the healing power of God is working for your son, that is a treatment.

"Ye shall seek me, and shall not find me," means that others may wonder what you are doing and be unable to follow you in understanding or belief. "And where I am, thither ye cannot come." Other members of your family, or the patient himself, may be unable to rise in consciousness and enter into the feeling of perfect health, because they are wrapped up in worldly beliefs. Quimby said that man's false belief is the sepulcher in which the wisdom of God is confined, and that the truth is the angel who rolls away the stone of superstition and ignorance, healing the mind and body.

The word "treatment" used in New Thought circles means the harmonious interaction and direction of the conscious and subconscious powers for a definite, specific purpose. In treating others or ourselves, we never identify with the disease. We have compassion for the person momentarily - "Yet a little while I am with you"; then we go to God and heaven, realizing the ideal perfection of the patient. The pharisaical beliefs (fear and doubt) cannot enter where confidence in God's power is. In prayer we are one with God, the only presence and power.

Here is an instance of how a woman applied this technique in the treatment of her child. Her child was very ill and hope of saving his life had been given up by all except the mother. She sat by the child's hospital bed and prayed as follows: "God is the life of my child, and His healing power is flowing through every atom of his being. The peace of God floods his mind and body, and through His power my child is made whole." She silently repeated this simple prayer over and over again, trying to lift up the idea of health in her mind. She knew intuitively and instinctively as she continued praying that she would reach the point of inner peace about her boy. After a few hours, the child began to cry for food. The doctor examined the child and said he had passed the crisis. She had realized the truth which set her child free.

Our reason and senses may question, ridicule, scoff, and laugh, but if we will only go within, knowing that when we feel something as true, Omnipotence moves in our behalf - then, though the whole world would deny it, we would demonstrate our desire, because we are sealed in faith. "According to your faith be it unto you."

The Miraculous Law of Healing

There is only one healing power. It is called by many names, such as God, Infinite Healing Presence, Nature, Divine Love, Divine Providence, the Miraculous Healing Power, Life, Life Principle, as well as many others. This knowledge goes back into the dim recesses of the past. An inscription has been found written over ancient temples which reads: "The doctor dresses the wound, and God heals the patient."

The healing presence of God is within you. No psychologist, minister, doctor, surgeon, priest, or psychiatrist heals anyone. For example, the surgeon removes a tumor, thereby removing the block and making way for the healing power of God to restore you. The psychologist or psychiatrist endeavors to remove the mental block and encourages the patient to adopt a new mental attitude which tends to release the Healing Presence, flowing through the patient as harmony, health, and peace. The minister asks you to forgive yourself and others and to get in tune with the Infinite by letting the healing power of love, peace, and goodwill flow through your subconscious mind, thereby cleansing all the negative patterns that may be lodged there.

This infinite healing presence of Life, which Jesus called "Father," is the healing agent in all diseases, whether mental, emotional, or physical.

This miraculous healing power in your subconscious mind, if scientifically directed, can heal your mind, body, and affairs of all disease and impediments. This healing power will respond to you regardless of your race, creed, or color. It does not care whether you belong to any church or whether you have any creedal affiliations or not. You have had hundreds of healings since you were a child. You can recall how this healing presence brought curative results to cuts, burns, bruises, contusions, sprains, etc., and, in all probability, like the author, you did not aid the healing in any way by the application of external remedies.

Healed of Spirit-Voices

A few years ago, a young man from a local university came to see me with the complaint that he was constantly hearing spirit-voices, that they made him do nasty things, and that they would not let him alone; neither would they permit him to read the Bible or other spiritual books. He was convinced that he was talking to supernatural beings.

This young man was clairaudient, and, not knowing that all men possess this faculty to some degree, he began to think it was due to evil spirits. His superstitious beliefs caused him to ascribe it to departed spirits. Through constant worry, he became a monomaniac on the subject. His subconscious mind, dominated and controlled by an all-potent but false suggestion, gradually took over control and mastery of his objective faculties, and his reason abdicated its throne. He was what you would call mentally unbalanced, as are all men who allow their false beliefs to obtain the ascendancy.

I explained to this university student that his subconscious mind is of tremendous importance and significance and that it can be influenced negatively and positively, but he had to make sure that he influenced it only positively, constructively, and harmoniously. The subconscious mind possesses transcendent powers, but it is at the same time amenable to good and bad suggestions. The explanation which I gave him made a profound impression on him.

I gave him the following written prayer which he was to repeat for ten or fifteen minutes three or four times a day:

> God's love, peace, harmony, and wisdom flood my mind
> and heart. I love the truth, I hear the truth, and I know the
> truth that God is Love, and His love surrounds me, enfolds
> me, and enwraps me. God's river of peace floods my mind,
> and I give thanks for my freedom.

He repeated this prayer slowly, quietly, reverently, and with deep feeling, particularly prior to sleep. By identifying himself with harmony and peace, he brought about a rearrangement of the thought-patterns and imagery of his mind, and a healing followed. He brought about a healing of his mind by repetition of these truths, coupled with faith and expectancy.

My own prayer for him night and morning was as follows: "John is thinking rightly. He is reflecting Divine wisdom and Divine intelligence in all his ways. His mind is the perfect mind of God, unchanging and eternal. He hears the voice of God, which is the inner voice of peace and love. God's river of peace governs his mind, and he is full of wisdom, poise, balance, and understanding. Whatever is vexing him is leaving him now, and I pronounce him free and at peace."

I meditated on these truths night and morning, getting the "feel" of peace and harmony; at the end of a week this young man was completely free and at peace.

She Wasn't Expected to Live

Some time ago, a woman told me that her child had a very high fever and was not expected to live. The doctor had prescribed small doses of aspirin and had administered an antibiotic preparation. The mother, who was involved in a contemplated divorce action, was terribly agitated and emotionally disturbed. This disturbed feeling was communicated subconsciously to the child, and naturally, the child got ill.

Children are at the mercy of their parents and are controlled by the dominant mental atmosphere and emotional climate of those around them. They have not yet reached the age of reason when they can take control of their own thoughts, emotions, and reactions to life.

The mother, at my suggestion, decided to become more at ease and relax her tensions by reading the 23rd Psalm, praying for guidance and for the peace and harmony of her husband. She poured out love and good will to him and overcame her resentment and inner rage. The fever of the child was due to the suppressed rage and anger of the mother, which was subjectively felt by the child and expressed as a high fever due to the excitation of the child's mind.

Having quieted her own mind, the mother began to pray for her child in this manner: "Spirit, which is God, is the life of my child. Spirit has no temperature; It is never sick or feverish. The peace of God flows through my child's mind and body. The harmony, health, love, and perfection of God are made manifest in every atom of my child's body now. She is relaxed and at ease, poised, serene, and calm. I am now stirring up the gift of God within her, and all is well."

She repeated the above prayer every hour for several hours. Shortly thereafter, she noticed a remarkable change in her child, who awakened and asked for a doll and something to eat. The temperature became normal. What had happened? The fever left the little girl because the mother was no longer feverish or agitated in her mind. Her mood of peace, harmony, and love was instantaneously felt by the child, and a corresponding reaction was produced.

The Natural-Born Healer

We are all "natural-born healers" for the simple reason that the healing presence of God is within all men, and all of us can contact It with our thoughts. It responds to all. This Healing Presence is in the dog, the cat, the tree, and the bird. It is omnipresent and is the life of all things.

Degrees of Faith

There are different degrees of faith. There is the man who, through faith, heals his ulcers, and another who heals a deep-seated, so-called incurable malignancy. It is as easy for the healing presence of God to heal a tubercular lung as it is to heal a cut on your finger. There is no great or small in the God that made us all; there is no big or little, no hard or easy. Omnipotence is within all men. The prayers of the man who lays his hand on another in order to induce a healing simply appeal to the cooperation of the patient's unconscious, whether the latter knows it or not, or whether he ascribes it to Divine intercession or not, and a response takes place; for according to the patient's faith is it done unto him.

A Case of Palsy

An old friend of mine in New York City suffered from palsy and tremors some years ago. His legs would become locked so that inability to move was experienced. Panic would ensue, and my friend would be frozen to the spot, even in the middle of a busy street. He got some mild relief from sedatives and antispasmodics which were prescribed by his physician; however, this condition of constant fear, panic, and foreboding was wearing him down. The following procedure was adopted.

The first step was to get him to see that there was a miraculous healing power within him which had made his body and which also could heal it. I suggested to him that he read the 5th Chapter of Luke, verses 18-24, and a related passage, Mark 2:3-5, where Jesus said to the man with the palsy: *"Man, thy sins are forgiven thee. I say unto thee, Arise, and take thy couch, and go into thine house."*

He read these verses avidly and was deeply moved by them. I explained to him that the couch or bed mentioned in the Bible means the bed in which a man lies in his own mind. The paralyzed man in the Bible undoubtedly was lying down amidst the thoughts of fear, doubt, condemnation, guilt, and superstition. These thoughts paralyze the mind and body.

We are told that Jesus healed the man of palsy by forgiving him his sins. To *sin* is to miss the mark, the goal of health, happiness, and peace. You forgive yourself by identifying mentally and emotionally with your ideal and continuing to do so until it gets within you as a conviction or subjective embodiment. You are sinning also when you think negatively or if you resent, hate, condemn, or engage in fear or worry. You are always sinning when you deviate or run away from your announced goal or aim in life, which should always be peace, harmony, wisdom, and perfect health -- the life more abundant.

My friend admitted to me that he was full of hatred toward a brother who had double-crossed him years ago in a financial deal. He also was full of guilt and self-condemnation, and he realized that, like the paralytic in the Bible, he could not be healed until his sins had been cancelled by simply forgiving himself and his brother. He admitted to himself that his physical condition was quite a problem, but that he didn't have to have it.

He turned to the healing presence of God within him and affirmed boldly:

"I fully and freely forgive myself for harboring negative and destructive thoughts, and I resolve to purify my mind from now on. I surrender and release my brother to God, and wherever he is, I sincerely wish for him health, happiness, and all the blessings of God. I am now aligned with the Infinite Healing Power, and I feel Divine love flowing through every atom of my being. I know that God's love is now permeating and saturating my whole body, making me whole and perfect. I sense the peace that passeth understanding. My body is a temple of the living God, and God is in His holy temple and I am free. As he meditated on these truths, he gradually became reconditioned to health and harmony. As he changed his mind, he changed his body. Changed attitudes change everything. Today he walks joyously and freely, completely healed."

He Healed His Withered Hand

An irate young man came to interview me, stating that his boss had fired him and had said to him, "You're like the man in the Bible with the withered hand." He said to me, "What did he mean? My hands are all right, they are perfectly normal." My explanation was as follows: In the correct interpretation of the Bible, it must be understood that principles are personified as persons in order to make portrayal and interaction vivid and forceful. We must not confine the story of the man with the withered hand to its literal meaning. The *hand* is a symbol of power, direction, and effectiveness. With your hand, you fashion, mold, direct, and design. Symbolically, a man has a withered hand when he has an inferiority complex and feels guilty and inadequate or is a defeatist. Such a man does not function efficiently and is not expressing his God-given powers.

This young man admitted that his dreams, ambitions, ideals, plans, and purposes were withered and frozen in his mind because he did not know how to bring them to pass. Not knowing the laws of mind and how to pray correctly, he found that his wonderful ideas died in his mind, resulting in frustration and neurosis. He was stagnating, literally dying on the vine. Furthermore, he was demoting and depreciating himself. His attitude toward life was all wrong; moreover, he admitted that his work was shoddy and desultory.

His hand (his ability to achieve and to accomplish) withered by saying to himself, "If I had Joe's brains or his wealth . . . his connections . . . I could advance and be somebody. But look at me, just a nobody. I was born on the wrong side of the tracks. I must he satisfied with my lot. I have a withered hand."

A remarkable change took place in this man, however, when he decided to *stretch forth his hand* by enlarging his concept and estimate of himself. He formed a picture in his mind of what he wished to achieve, i.e., to direct a large organization and to be successful. He began to affirm frequently: "I can do all things, through the God-power which strengthens, guides, controls, and directs me. I realize that I am going where my vision is. I now turn with faith and confidence to the Infinite Intelligence within me, knowing that I am directed by an inner wisdom. I know in my heart that the Godpower flows through the patterns of thought and imagery in my mind, and I am under a Divine compulsion to succeed."

As he identified himself mentally and emotionally with these new concepts, he went forward from promotion to promotion and is now general manager of a large corporation, his current salary exceeding $75,000 annually.

How the Hopeless Case Was Healed

Jesus commanded the dead man, *"Young man, I say unto thee, Arise. And he that was dead sat up and began to speak"* (Luke 7:14-15).

When it says *the dead man sat up and began to speak,* it means that when your prayer is answered you speak in a new tongue of joyous health, and you exude an inner radiance. Your dead hopes and desires speak when you bear witness to your inner beliefs and assumptions.

As a corollary to this, I would like to tell about a young man I saw in Ireland a few years ago. He is a distant relative. He was in a comatose condition; his kidneys had not functioned for three days. His condition had been pronounced hopeless when I went to see him, accompanied by one of his brothers. I knew that he was a devout Catholic, and I said to him, "Jesus is right here, and you see him. He is putting his hand out and is this moment laying his hand upon you."

I repeated this several times, slowly, gently, and positively. He was unconscious when I spoke and was not consciously aware of either of us. He sat up in bed, however, opened his eyes, and said to both of us, "Jesus was here; I know I am healed I shall live."

What had happened? This man's subconscious mind had accepted my statement that Jesus was there, and his subconscious projected that thought-form, i.e. this man's concept of Jesus was portrayed based on what he saw in church statues, paintings, etc. He believed that Jesus was there in the flesh and that he had placed his hands upon him.

The readers of my book, *The Power of Your Subconscious Mind,* are well aware of the fact that you can tell a man who is in a trance that his grandfather is here now and that he will see him clearly. He will see what he believes to be his grandfather. His subconscious reveals the image of his grandfather based on his subconscious memory picture. You can give the same man a posthypnotic suggestion by saying to him, "When you come out of this trance, you will greet your grandfather and talk to him," and he will do exactly that. This is called a subjective hallucination.

The faith which was kindled in the unconscious of my Catholic relative, based on his *firm belief* that Jesus came to heal him, was the healing factor. It is always done unto us according to our faith, mental conviction, or just blind belief. His subconscious mind was amenable to my suggestion; his deeper mind received and acted upon the idea I had implanted in his mind. In a sense, you could call such an incident *the resurrection of the dead*. It was the resurrection of his health and vitality. According to his belief was it done unto him.

Blind Faith and True Faith

True faith is based on the knowledge of the way your conscious and subconscious mind functions and on the combined harmonious functioning of these two levels of mind scientifically directed. Blind faith is healing without any scientific understanding whatsoever of the forces involved. The voodoo doctor or witch doctor in the jungles of Africa heals by faith, and so do the bones of dogs (believed to be the bones of saints by the believer), or anything else which moves man's mind from fear to faith.

In all instances - regardless of the technique, *modus operandi* process, incantation, or invocation offered to saints and spirits - it is the subconscious mind that does the healing. Whatever you believe is operative instantly in your subconscious mind.

Be like the little eight-year-old boy in our Sunday school. Eye drops were not clearing up his eye infection, and he prayed as follows: "God, you made my eyes. I demand action, I want healing now. Hurry up. Thank you." He had a remarkable healing because of his simplicity, spontaneity, and childlike faith *in God. "Go and do thou likewise" (Luke 10:37).*

How to Give a Spiritual Treatment

Spiritual treatment means that you turn to the Indwelling God and remind yourself of His peace, harmony, wholeness, beauty, boundless love, and limitless power. Know that God loves you and cares for you. As you pray this way the fear gradually will fade away. If you pray about a heart condition, do not think of the organ as diseased as this would not be spiritual thinking. Thoughts are things. Your spiritual thought takes the form of cells, tissues, nerves, and organs. To think of a damaged heart or high blood pressure tends to suggest more of what you already have. Cease dwelling on symptoms, organs or any part of the body. Turn your mind to God and His love. Feel and know that there is only one healing Presence and Power, and to its corollary: *There is no Power to challenge the action of God.*

Quietly and lovingly affirm that: The uplifting, healing, strengthening power of the healing Presence is flowing through you making you every whit whole. Know and feel that the harmony, beauty, and life of God manifest themselves in you as strength, peace, vitality, wholeness, and right action. Get a clear realization of this, and the damaged heart or other disease organ will be cured in the light of God's love.

"Glorify God in your body" (I Corinthians 6:20) organs will be cured in the light of God's love."

Very Profitable Pointers

1. The healing power of God is within you. Remove any mental block and let the healing power flow through you.

2. A monomaniac is a man who permits his mind to be dominated and controlled by an all-potent but false suggestion.

3. When a mother is agitated and seething with inner turmoil and rage, this negative emotion is communicated to the subconscious of her child and can cause fever. Let God's river of peace flood the mind and heart, and the child's fever will abate and harmony will be restored.

4. All of us are natural-born healers because the Infinite Healing Presence is within us, and we can contact It with our thoughts and beliefs.

5. The miraculous healing power which made your body knows how to heal it. It knows all the processes and functions of your body. Trust the healing power and accept a healing now.

6. You can recondition yourself to health and harmony as you meditate frequently on harmony, vitality, wholeness, beauty, and perfection.

7. In the Bible, principles are personified as persons in order to make portrayal and interaction vivid and forceful. You can overcome a feeling of inferiority by joining up with God and by sensing that one with God is a majority.

8. There are no incurable diseases. There are incurable people who believe they can't be healed, and according to their belief is it done unto them.

9. Faith healing is healing without any scientific understanding of the forces involved. Spiritual mind healing is the combined and harmonious functioning of your conscious and subconscious mind, scientifically directed for a specific purpose. In all instances, it is the subconscious mind that heals regardless of the technique or process used.

How You Can Face the Word "Incurable" in Your Own Life

Don't let the word "incurable" frighten you. Realize that you are dealing with the Creative Intelligence which made your body and that, although some men will say that a healing is impossible, be assured that this infinite Healing Presence is instantly available, and you can always draw on its power through the creative law of your own mind. Make use of this power now and perform miracles in your life. Remember that a miracle cannot prove that which is impossible; it is a confirmation of that which is possible, for *"with God all things are possible"* (Matthew 19:26). *"I will restore health unto thee, and I will heal thee of thy wounds, saith the Lord"* (Jeremiah 30:17).

The word "Lord" in the Bible means the creative law of your mind. There is a deep-lying, healing principle which permeates the entire universe, that flows through your mental patterns, images, and choices, and objectifies them in form. You can bring into your life anything you wish through this infinite healing principle which operates through your own mind.

You may use this universal healing principle for any particular purpose. It is not confined to healing of the mind or body. It is the same principle which attracts to you the ideal husband or wife, prospers you in business, finds for you your true place in life, and reveals answers to your most difficult problems. Through the correct application of this principle, you can become a great salesman, musician, physician, or surgeon. You can use it to bring harmony where discord exists, peace to supplant pain, joy in place of sadness, and abundance in place of poverty.

Healing of Dropsy

I knew a man in London, England, who was not only very religious but was completely free from any ill will or resentment. However, he saw his father die of dropsy, and it made a very deep and lasting impression on him; he told me that all his life since that event, he feared that the same thing would happen to him. He also told me that his father, by way of treatment, used to be tapped with an instrument, and that the doctor would draw out large amounts of water from his abdominal area. This lingering fear, which was never neutralized, was undoubtedly the cause of his dropsical condition. He did not know the simple psychological truth which Dr. Phineas Parkhurst Quimby of Maine had elucidated about one hundred years ago. Dr. Quimby said that *if you believe something, it will manifest, whether you are consciously thinking of it or not.* This man's fear grew into a conviction that he would become a victim of the same disorder that had troubled his father. This explanation, however, helped the man considerably. He began to realize that he had accepted a lie as truth.

I pointed out to him that his fear was a perversion of the truth, a fear which had no real power because there is no principle behind disease. There is a principle of health, none of disease; a principle of abundance, none of poverty; a principal of honesty, none of deceit; a principle of mathematics, none of error; and a principle of beauty, none of ugliness. Fortunately, his belief was in the only power which controlled him, and he knew that his mind could be used negatively or positively.

He came to a definite conclusion in his mind by reasoning that the Healing Presence which made him was still with him and that his disease was due to a disordered group of disease-soaked thoughts; thus he rearranged his mind to conform to the Divine pattern of harmony, health, and wholeness.

Before going to sleep at night, he would affirm with feeling and with deep meaning behind each word: "The Healing Presence is now going to work, transforming, healing, restoring, and controlling all processes of my body according to Its wisdom and Divine nature. My entire system is cleansed, purified, and quickened by the vitalizing energy of God. Divine circulation, assimilation, and elimination operate in my mind and body. The joy of the Lord is my abiding strength. I am made every whit whole, and I give thanks."

He repeated this prayer every night for about thirty days. At the end of that time, his mind had reached a conviction of health, and his physician dismissed him as whole and perfect.

Steps in Healing

The first step in healing is not to be afraid of the manifest condition - from this very moment. The second step is to realize that the condition is only the product of past thinking, which will have no more power to continue its existence. The third step is mentally to exalt the miraculous healing power of God within you.

This procedure instantly will stop the production of all mental poisons in you or in the person for whom you are praying. Live in the embodiment of your desire, and your thought and feeling will soon be made manifest. Do not allow yourself to be swayed by human opinion and worldly fears, but live emotionally in the belief that it is God in action in your mind and body.

Spiritual Blindness

Millions of people are "blind," i.e., they are psychological and spiritually "blind" because they do not know that they become what they think all day long. Man is spiritually and mentally "blind" when he is hateful, resentful, or envious of others. He does not know that he is actually secreting mental poisons which tend to destroy him.

Thousands of people are constantly saying that there is no way to solve their problems, and their situation is hopeless. Such an attitude is the result of spiritual blindness. Man begins to see spiritually and mentally when he gets a new understanding of his mental powers and develops a conscious awareness that the wisdom and intelligence in his subconscious can solve all his problems.

Everyone should become aware of the inter-relationship and interaction of the conscious and subconscious mind. Persons who were once blind to these truths, after careful introspection, will now begin to see the vision of health, wealth, happiness, and peace of mind that can be theirs through the correct application of the laws of mind.

Vision is Spiritual, Eternal, and Indestructible.

We do not create vision, rather we manifest or release it. We see through the eye, not with it. The cornea of the eye is stimulated by light waves from objects in space; through the optic nerve, these stimuli are carried to the brain. When the inner light, or intelligence, meets the outer light in this manner, by a process of interpretation, we see.

Your eyes symbolize Divine love and a delight in the ways of God, plus a hunger and thirst for God's truth. Your *right eye* symbolizes right thought and right action. The left eye symbolizes God's love and wisdom. Think right and radiate good will to all, and you will focus perfectly.

Receive thy sight . . . And immediately he received his sight, and followed him, glorifying God (Luke 18:42-43).

Special Prayer for Eyes and Ears

I am the Lord that healeth me. My vision is spiritual, eternal, and a quality of my consciousness. My eyes are Divine ideas, and they are always functioning perfectly.

My perception of spiritual Truth is clear and powerful. The light of understanding dawns in me; I see more and more of God's Truth every day. I see spiritually; I see mentally; I see physically. I see images of Truth and Beauty everywhere.

The infinite Healing Presence is now, this moment, rebuilding my eyes. They are perfect, Divine instruments, enabling me to receive messages from the world within and the world without. The glory of God is revealed in my eyes.

I hear the Truth; I love the Truth; I know the Truth. My ears are God's perfect ideas, functioning perfectly at all times. My ears are the perfect instruments which reveal God's harmony to me. The love, beauty, and harmony of God flow through my eyes and ears; I am in tune with the Infinite. I hear the still, small voice of God within me. The Holy Spirit quickens my hearing, and my ears are open and free.

Eight Healing Steps

1. Man says it's impossible, but with God all things are possible. You can be healed by God, Who created you.

2. The healing principle flows through your mental patterns of thought and imagery, bringing all things you wish into manifestation.

3. If you believe something, it will be manifest - whether or not you are consciously thinking of it. Believe only in that which heals, blesses, and inspires you.

4. Exalt the power of God in the midst of you, and you will stop the spread of any disease in your body.

5. The thankful heart is close to God. Let all your prayers be made known with praise and thanksgiving.

6. You are spiritually blind when you don't know that thoughts are things, that what you feel you attract, and that what you imagine, you become.

7. Vision is spiritual, eternal, and indestructible. A wonderful prayer for the eyes is to affirm regularly: "I see better spiritually, mentally, and physically."

8. *"I will lift up mine eyes unto the hills, from whence cometh my help"* (Psalm 121:1).

www.ingramcontent.com/pod-product-compliance
Lightning Source LLC
LaVergne TN
LVHW041809190726
843493LV00009B/2848